Forest Music

Also by Susan Connolly
How High the Moon (with Catherine Phil MacCarthy)
For the Stranger
Race to the Sea
Winterlight

with Anne-Marie Moroney:
Race to the Sea
Ogham: Ancestors Remembered in Stone
Stone and Tree Sheltering Water
Winterlight

Forest Music

SUSAN CONNOLLY

Shearsman Books

Published in the United Kingdom in 2009 by
Shearsman Books Ltd
58 Velwell Road
Exeter EX4 4LD

www.shearsman.com

ISBN 978-1-84861-026-2
First Edition

Acknowledgements
Some of these poems have appeared in *Books Ireland, Women's Work, Race
to the Sea, The Stony Thursday Book, Drogheda Writes, Southword, Revival,
Crannóg, The SHOp, Jones Av.* (Canada), *Cyphers, Orbis, Stone and Tree
Sheltering Water, Poetry Ireland Review, Ogham, Winterlight, Áit Bhríde, The
Drogheda Independent, Dowth: Winter Sunsets, Electric Acorn, Thornfield, Irish
Studies Review, Boyne Berries, Shearsman, A Salmon in the Pool, Poems of Oriel*
and *Something Beginning With P.*

'Newgrange' and 'Dowth' have been set to music by the composer
Michael Holohan.

Thanks to The Patrick and Katherine Kavanagh Trust, The Heinrich Böll
Committee, Drogheda Borough Council and the staff of the Tyrone
Guthrie Centre, Annaghmakerrig.

Thanks to John Moloney and Breffni Murphy for their help with the layout
of some of the poems in 'Walking the Seawall' and 'Monasterboice'.

Thanks to Thornfield Poets and WEB.

I would like to thank Louise C. Callaghan, Anne-Marie Moroney, Alison
Kelly, Patricia Lysaght and Marie MacSweeney for their helpful readings
of many of the poems; Edel Robinson and Michael Holohan for much
discussion late into the night about the High Crosses at Monasterboice; Lia
Mills for her friendship and support over the years.

CONTENTS

Forest Music

One thousand autumn oak leaves   11
Piano Lessons   12
Brigit   15
A Gift of Words   18
Butterfly   19
Winterlight   20
Forest Music   21
A Salmon in the Pool   22
In Memory of Bettina Poeschel   23
The Path   24
A Small Red Leaf   25
The Maiden Tower   26
The Cobbled Garden   30
Brú na Bóinne   34
    Newgrange
    Knowth
    Dowth
First Love   36
Old House   37
Líadan   39
Francis Ledwidge   40
Raising Ructions   41
The Biology Lab   43
The Deer's Cry   45
Ogham   47
Avittoria   50
Kilnasaggart Pillar Stone   51
I have had enough   53
Alone, Not Alone   54
Today With You   55
Female Figure   56
Tobar an tSolais   58

The Wound   59
Boa Janus   60
Coney Hall, 1880   62
Fedelm's Reply to Medb   64
A Shooting Star   65
The Woody Island   66
The Stillness of Trees   68
Poll na bPéist   69
Father-in-Law   70

Walking the Seawall
Mirrors   73
Many Selves   75
Like Leaves on a Tree   76
Toberfinn   77
Ladywell, Slane   78
Songs of Amergin   80
Walking the Seawall at Baltray   83
The Five Roads at Tara   84
Cormorant   86
Rose 1   87
Rose 2   88
Carnations   89
Edel   90
At a Terry Riley Concert   91
St. Stephen's Night   93
Sandwaves   94
Haiku   96

Monasterboice
The Cross of Muiredach   101
The West Cross   102
Dextera Dei   103
Names for a High Cross   104
Christ in the Arms of this Cross   105
Around the Cross   106

FOREST MUSIC

for Michael, Breifne and Líadan

Céol caille
fom-chanad . . .
la fogur fairrge flainne.

Forest music
sang to me . . .
and the sound of the reddening sea.

One thousand autumn oak leaves

One thousand autumn oak leaves
sweep coldly down the path
that's brought you to this day.
Every muscle in your body
warns of a storm brewing.

Get up. Step outside.
Take a deep breath.
Don't you know
you are a garden
you are always digging?

One thousand autumn oak leaves,
ten thousand memories.
Choose one to hold you still
while the sun weaves
light out of darkness.

Why turn your back on everything?
Why this bitter storm?
Everything that's brought you
to this day is like a song
you want to hear.

Now listen to another song,
all that has yet to happen,
all that patiently
waits for you, beyond
eye, ear, tongue.

PIANO LESSONS

1. Mrs. MacAllister

Early September, first lesson
with Mrs. MacAllister:
'Let me hear you play.
Play your favourite piece for me.'
Shy, shaky, in slow motion
I try *The Sunbeam Polka*.
She nods and smiles.
I notice her mansize hands,
the kindness in her voice.

Tuesday lunchtime, Mrs. MacAllister:
my name on a brand new
Grade III book.
She plays six pieces.
'Choose three you like.'
We begin: right hand, left hand,
hands together, fingering.
'Though the notes are important,
feeling is everything.'

2. Piano Lessons

Notes fall beneath my hands
like flame-coloured leaves.
I want to play with them,
to catch, kick, scatter
and gather them.
Eleven years old, homesick,
I crave the familiar.

Christmas over, hands
and heart numb,
one Tuesday lunchtime
I begin Bartók's
Slovakian Folk Tune.
The first chord sends
a shiver up my spine.

I glance sideways
at Mrs. MacAllister:
'Did I play the right notes?'
'That's a minor seventh
chord,' she says.
'I'll change
the fingering for you.'

What a strange sound
I hold captive in my hands.
What luck to reach out
and find exactly
what I need!
At home at last in the new
and unfamiliar.

My life a piece of music
I have barely begun
to play, week by week
Mrs. MacAllister draws out
the silence at my core.
Teacher and child
each Tuesday lunchtime

side by side,
with a sudden pang I know—
that's my favourite piece of all.

Memory which lightens
and brightens everything.
Heartwarming, comforting
music at my core.

BRIGIT

1.

Run, little fox,
past hermit cell
and derelict castle,
past river and monastery
and quaint rose cottage.
Through oak wooded
centuries
weaving your way—
run swiftly now
in the open air.

Brigit called a wild fox
out of the forest.
That fox was you!
You played for a while
and went safe
through the forest,
the king on his horse
after you.

Brigit hung her wet robe
to dry on a ray of sun.
If they touched
her shadow
the sick were healed.
'Every stranger is Christ,'
she said, and gave
to everyone.

People came to visit her.
A playful fox drew near.

She believed in mercy.
In the doorway of her
mother's house at sunrise
Brigit was born.
A fox howled
the day she died.

2.

Brigit—
we name our daughters
after you,
Brigit, Breege, Breda.
After our mothers, sisters
friends
we call our daughters
Bríd, Bridie, Biddy.

Daylight will be cold
if your name fades
from our lips,
like a fire gone out
forever.

At the edge of Cuan wood
the fox goes,
no king of Leinster with him now,
though the same land
stretches away.

Brigit—
bright stillness in the sky
while I live stormily
below—

bright spark within

Brigit búadach
Bethad beo. *

for Alison Kelly

*Victorious Brigit,
The living one of life.

A Gift of Words

Because you followed
pain to its source,
led by its wail
deep into a forest

where you found me
hurt, my life a trap
snapped shut
upon me—

perhaps all
you have gained
is this reaching out,
another's pain

to comprehend,
and a gift of words:
this conversation
between us.

In their own way
two wild yet gentle animals
have also been set free:
trust and friendliness.

At the forest's edge
they hesitate, hollow-eyed,
wait for the right moment
to follow us.

BUTTERFLY

Today
peace alighted
like a butterfly
on my right hand.

I kept still
as a twig
or a branch
so I could enjoy
from close up
this rare moment.

WINTERLIGHT

I'll comb the beach at Seapoint,
until I find the finest shell,
and I'll give it to you to keep.

I'll walk alone in Beaulieu Wood,
and every leaf on every tree
will tremble with your laughter.

At *Brú na Bóinne* I'll tell you
stories about Oenghus and Caer,
and I'll tell you one about me.

I'll endure the dark for a night
and a day, ransacking my heart
for the poem you need to hear.

Then, it will be like standing
with you inside *Caiseal Oenghusa*,
as the midwinter sun begins to rise.

Even to remember ourselves
touched by that winterlight, will
drive out loneliness forever.

Forest Music

The intricate
pathways
of my life
have led me
to inhabit
a deep forest
sadness.

But lulled
today
by forest
music, I knew
for a while
what really
matters.

A Salmon in the Pool

A map full of poems,
words instead of roads.
A knot untangled
in each poet's heart.

I give you this map.
You know how
heart and reason
were snatched away
one night.
Life seemed
a stagnant pool
I needed to escape.

You teach me
to retrieve my life,
something difficult
to catch
as the magic salmon
in the pool.

Slowly the murky pool
comes clear:
I see my past,
my present.

Sometimes I nearly catch
the salmon.
I imagine the taste,
what I will see.

In Memory of Bettina Poeschel

The Boyne flows ever deeper
for all that it has seen

but fate struck fast as lightning
one bright September morning

before we knew your name
or what you looked like

or how you would be found,
your glasses smashed beside you.

Your cry skimmed the river,
petrified its depths.

The Boyne stood still a moment,
then slowly turned away.

Bettina Poeschel was a visitor from Munich who was abducted in
September 2001 while walking from Drogheda to the Brú na Bóinne
Interpretive Centre. Her body was found three weeks later.

THE PATH

If I were a child again,
if I could see ahead,
I might see someone
who looks like me,
who would like
to talk with me.

She'd tell me
not to worry.
From where she is
she can see
my life
will be alright.

A clear path ahead
she sees:
days and nights
when I feel
safe, lonely,
reckless.

My life has to be
exactly as it is,
so that she can find
her way back
step by step,
to talk with me.

A Small Red Leaf

A year like a book
with a page ripped out.
A chapter of my life.
The missing page
marked by
a small red leaf.
The torn page folded,
warm in my pocket.

A page that can shine
like the sun
over my whole life
and help me see,
must be
very important . . .
a crossroads
where hope,
despair, cruelty
and kindness
have met, mingled—
given birth
to something new.

Maybe soon
I will take that book,
find the small red leaf,
put back
the missing page.

An important page.
An important year.
Perfect, mysterious
as a small red leaf.

THE MAIDEN TOWER

Built in the reign of Elizabeth I
to commemorate her celibacy

1.

Standing alone
in the evening light,
its austere, withdrawn air
affects me.
So alone by the river.
Twelve feet square,
eighty feet high;
at its centre
a winding stair.
The whole structure
built to serve
the flagged platform
at the top.
For centuries a landmark,
a beacon for sailing ships.
A watchtower.
But once for a woman
it became home
and hermit cell.

2.

In the spring of 1819
the people of Bettystown
saw smoke coming from the top
of Maiden Tower.

Curious, they found there
a careworn, ageing woman.
For a bed she had gathered
an armful of marram grass.

She had lit a fire,
and to this place
dragged a spinning wheel.
Here she spun her flax.

'I am tired,' she said.
'In a dream I was told
to come here
and struggle no more.

'This is my answer
to friends who left me.
Here I will live
and die.'

She seldom left her high home
except on Sundays
when she came down
to hear Mass at Mornington.

There at the altar
this neatly dressed woman
offered for the poor
the linen of her labour.

She told her visitors
she was from Drogheda—
'But I left that place
where I outlived my affections.'

Spring and summer of 1819
sped. Winter
once more asserted
its icy control.

A gentleman nearby
out of pity
made sure
she lacked nothing.

Sailors crossing the sand-bar
saw her candle
lit to welcome them home.
It warmed their hearts.

So she weathered
another winter,
was glad of another spring
and summer.

Then Mr. Brabazon died.
Health and spirit
weakening,
she left the tower.

3.

Loopholes of light and air
as I climb the limestone
spiral stair.
Children play
a dangerous game here.
Over the battlements
jumpers fly.

Climbing, I think of you,
old mendicant:
patronised by the rich
you worked
for the poor.
Your weaving,
transcendental.

I don't even know your name.

What kind of friends
drove you to this place?

Your footsteps and your silence
echo—
as if I were the tower
you climbed one day,
in search of home.

THE COBBLED GARDEN

1.

The stone garden
vanishes with its maker,
like a wave
sinking back to sea.
Yet under moss,
stones, clay
the garden waits,
till we discover it
one day.
　　　South-facing
and still the best place
to sit in the sun.

Like a tree-stump
the low pillar juts out.
We start to dig,
not knowing
we will find cobbles
set carefully across
the garden's width,
and five feet
lengthways.

At the centre,
a heart of small
yellow stones
lies within a herring-bone
wreath of bigger
grey stones,
all brought
from the beach.

On the left,
N-O-V.
On the right,
the impossible—
'bicycle wheels',
till a child
runs his fingers
round the woven pattern:
'Look! One-eight-three-three!'
Suddenly we can see:
November 1833.

Outside the wreath
lines lead north,
due south,
east and west.
The heart is damaged.
A heavy round ornament
embedded there—
then removed,
has left its mark.

We swear we will cycle
out to sea,
find the yellow stones
that match.
We will rebuild
this heart, one hundred
and sixty years old.

But summer ends.
The back door
slams shut
on the garden.
A door between us

closes, changing
our lives.

2.

Two years later
at Easter
I open the door,
step outside,
examine the moss-covered
cobbles.

A date written
in the ground
leads me to start digging
whenever the sun shines.
Removing moss
with toothbrush
and trowel,
gradually I lay bare
another woman's
labour of love.

Her spirit
has possessed me.
I follow in her path,
commemorating
in stone
something beyond words.

Every morning now,
since I cleared
the garden,
I wake to the sound
of a thrush

breaking snail shells
on the hard cobbles.

Later,
sweeping away
the empty shells,
I hear the surge
of the sea
over yellow stones
one hundred
and sixty years ago.

She gathered them,
brought them home,
made a portrait
of her brimming heart.

If she knew
how much I love
her garden
she would smile.

And smile again to see
the cobbled heart
shimmer in the sun today,
mirroring mine.

Happy.
Capable of embracing
everything.

BRÚ NA BÓINNE

1. *Newgrange*

If I stay away too long
you call me back,
Brú na Bóinne,
and I plunge deeper
into myself.
Then you send me out
to the world again,
imbued with death
and darkness.

I spend the days
alone here, turning
death into life.
Let every step
bring me closer to you,
Brú na Bóinne,
along my path of light.

2. *Knowth*

The little wren
shadowed us,
flitting from
stone to
sunlit stone.
So tame
he made us smile.
He reminded me
of words

buried deep
within.
I wanted them
to be like him.
Afraid of no one.

3. Dowth

Bright leaves falling,
hide a darker world.

I hear them whisper:
'Let her sleep.'

Bright leaves silent
at my feet.

I waken to
this darker world.

FIRST LOVE

You at the Blüthner composing,
the freezing piano room yours.
The navy fingerless gloves you wore,
your tea-stained Egyptian mug.

Lighting a fire in November,
pulling my table closer.
Books like flowers around me.
Settling down to write.

Words and music led us astray,
travelling different roads.
Night feasts beside the fire.
Stories to tell. Then bed.

Running to catch the bus to Dublin,
chasing after the last bus home.
A big house in chaos.
Life balancing on stilts.

One day our sky blue dresser
fell off its rickety legs.
Your favourite mug lay broken
there on the floor of our lives.

Leafing through the dictionary,
searching, searching for words.
Playing the piano over and over,
sounding at last your chords.

Old House

'The house where we sat
  on the back wall
    playing *I spy*.
The house of *my* room,
  the *old* room
  and the *other* room.
Downstairs
  to the bathroom,
    upstairs
to the kitchen,
  the back door
  miles away.
The piano room
  my favourite.
    Remember
the flood in the lower
  surgery—where
  we kept our bikes?'

'I remember the great
  Christmas parties
    in the waiting room,
the train screeching
  and looping around
  the big table—
but it was a cold, dark
  room.
    The surgery
was the junk room.
  I loved exploring
  there, playing with
my cast-off toys.'

'Remember the ghost
    in the cellar?'
'Yes, and I remember
    the great games of
    hide and seek.'

'Where?' 'In the garden,
    over the wall,
        everywhere.
It was the perfect house.
    It had everything
    of my dreams—
but in the end
    it became too much
        for us.
It was big,
    it was old,
    it was caving in
on top of us.
    So we gave
        our house to
somebody else
    to mind.
        And we left.'

LÍADAN

a poet of the 7th century

Five main roads converge at Tara,
monks live on tiny islands,
Newgrange lies tumbledown.

Líadan and Cuirithir hear:
the lulling song of the forest,
the roar of a flame-red sea.

Francis Ledwidge

A five-acre garden, apples, cherries,
Sunday crowds at ease.
Children laughing, blackbirds
sleeping, cherry-drunk.

Matt's fiddle calms you,
your thoughts read at a glance.
You walk the tangled roads
round Slane, dreaming of Ellie.

Homesick in Gallipoli.
Home-rivers wonder where you are.
Killed by shrapnel at Ypres.
Empty roads are grieving.

Matt's grave at Donaghmore,
Ellie's, on the Hill of Slane.
At Rossnaree I saw you,
sleeping by the Boyne.

Raising Ructions

for Lia Mills

We didn't know it then,
but the moment we set off
on our separate paths
away from each other—
the great search began,
like roots reaching down
into dark, damp earth,
roots no one could see,
least of all, ourselves.

One night someone
spoke your name,
asked if I knew you.
In silence
I looked at a full moon.
Then something missing
for many years
clicked back into place,
and I felt at peace.

Remembering two girls
who set up obstacles
on the school stage
and spent hours
jumping over them,
I saw how well
we took care of each other,
making the most
of a bad thing.

Running riot,
raising ructions, barred
from speaking—
we sent notes.
We sought each other out,
put down roots
to steady our spirits
wherever
we might roam.

Back then
we felt that we were
playthings of the gods,
at their mercy,
prey to every little whim.
We learned from them
a simple lesson:
how to wrest fun
out of our lives.

I see us still—
two girls on a stage,
and remember the night
two paths converged
under moonlight
at the mention of your name,
I silently thinking:
How high the moon,
how very high the moon!

THE BIOLOGY LAB

Early summer,
early evening,
I am alone.
Daygirls gone.
Boarders in another
building.
Silence.
But nothing like
the silence
between them
and me.
I stand, a blade
in my right hand.
Body imbued
with power,
the only power
left to me.
I think nothing,
know only
the silent build-up
to this.
No one knows
anything about me.
I want to see blood.
My blood.
It is the moment
before the axe
strikes a tree.
Blood flows,
a river running
out to sea.

On empty beaches
everywhere,
waves break
in their endless
turmoil.
But in myself
now
I hear
what is hidden,
peaceful, close.

THE DEER'S CRY

Patrick said this after King Laoghaire
set out from Tara to kill him

I have lit the holy fire
and you are angry,
but I am peaceful
as the white deer grazing
in the woods at Slane.
  Brightness of sun
    whiteness of snow
      splendour of fire
We do not know each other
but we will meet soon.
We are like two hills
on either side of the river.
  Speed of lightning
    sea-depth
      firmness of rock
Some may go in chariots,
and some on horses,
but I walk in the name
            of my God.
  God's wisdom guide me
  God's word speak for me
  God's path before me
Your chariots cross the Boyne;
you want to destroy
the living fire.
                I sing:
  Christ where I lie
    Christ where I sit
      Christ where I rise

I sing:
Christ in every eye that sees me
Christ in every ear that hears me

Who makes you think
that I and my monks
are eight wild deer
entering the woods at Slane
with the fawn, Benen,
following?

for Michael

Ogham

CUNAMAQQI CORBBI MAQQI:
(stone) of Conn
son of Corb
son of . . .

MAQILIAGMAQIERCA:
(stone) of Maqi-liag
son of Erca

DOVETI MAQQI CATTINI:
friends—
leave my name intact!
I am Dovetos
son of Cattinos

Strokes and notches
climb tall stone.
Lines in sets of five
or less
thud across the edge.
Finger-alphabet.
Frozen invocation

**CUNAMAQQI CORBBI MAQQI
MUCCOI DOVVINIAS:**
Conn, son of Corb
of Duibhne

The Christians
defacing us
we write 'Mu-',
say the missing name
in our minds:

BROCAGNI MAQI MU-

Invoke my name!
Place your fingers
in the ice-cold notches.
Hear me speak

Remember Dovetos
your ancestor

    ★

Hand-signals
caught in stone—
magical inscription:
AKEVRITTI

Christian sledgehammers
smash away **DOVVINIAS.**
They turn me
upside down,
my god-ancestor
buried in earth

MAQQI MUCCOI
under taboo—
we garble **GAQIMU,**
GUCOI;
VEQREQ MOQOI GLUNLEGGET:
Fiachra, descendant
of 'Glunlegget'

As if they covered
nakedness
they write over us:

QRIMITER RONANN MAQ COMOGANN:
Ronán, the priest son
of Comgán

The Sign of the Cross
surrounds my stone—
two on each side
but on the north
just one,
the way left open
'for demons to escape'

With pin-scrapes
and scratches
on a stone
eleven feet high,
in miniature
we reply

**MAQQI-IARI KOI MAQQI MUCCOI
DOVVINIAS**

AVITTORIA

the only Ogham monument
to commemorate a woman

Once a step
in the path
to a church

Now I lie
in a locked chest
inside the church

AVITTORIGES
INIGENA CUNIGNI

I would love
to stand where hills
cover my bones

To feel the rain
finger my name.

Traveller
drawn to
Carmarthenshire—
lift the heavy lid!

Shine on me
again,
bright sun—

Avittoria,
daughter of Cunignos

Kilnasaggart Pillar Stone

inloc
sotani
mmairni
ternohc
macceran
bicercul
peterap
 stel

★★

in loc

so tani

mmairni

ternohc

mac ceran

bic er cul

peter ap

 stel

in loc

so tani

mmairni

Ternoc

mac ceran bic

er cul

Peter

 apostle

in loc so
tanimmairni
Ternoc
son of Ciaran
the little
er cul
Peter the
Apostle

this place
tanimmairni
Ternoc
son of Ciaran the little
er
the protection of
Peter the
Apostle

**

Ternoc
son of Ciaran the Little
bequeathed
this site
in return for
the protection of
Peter the
Apostle

I HAVE HAD ENOUGH

I have had enough
sadness,
enough of the sad
rattle of shells
and stones
dragged
back and forth
each day
by the rising,
receding tides.
It is time
to gather up
those memories
lost in my depths;
memories delicate
as shells,
enduring as stone.
I will wash them
ashore, sweep them
higher than
any tide.
I will carry them
home,
be proud of them.
They are all I have
to help me know
when the sadness
began.

ALONE, NOT ALONE

Sometimes
I need to be alone
to hear what troubles me.
Alone as in sleep.
Free to think and dream.
Like a train
the dark feeling
approaches,
carries me away.

Sometimes
I become very quiet
when you say
you are not alone
anymore.
Like two rivers
I can hear our lives,
one flowing
into the other.

TODAY WITH YOU

Today with you
was like sitting
alone,
quietly reading
my favourite
book of poetry.
Book with a
wonderful title,
yielding up
new treasure
each time
I turn its pages.
Treasure of
startling beauty.
Pages loved
till threadbare.
Today with you:
complete
contentment.
Quietly
reading you,
like a book
of poetry.

FEMALE FIGURE

Sheela-na-gig, White Island, Lough Erne

Mouth fixed
in a wide grin,
puffed-out
cheeks
fingers to lips—
am I saying
something bad?
No! after
centuries of
darkness
I tell
the truth.

Women—
you look at me
and talk about
your 'desire-need'.
I hear a babble,
then your
wisdom.
Fingers to
lips I speak
my need of
you.

Eyes framed
by a heavy ridge
I laugh—
witness
and survivor.

Caught in stone
I celebrate
all who tell
the truth—
over centuries
of darkness.

TOBAR AN TSOLAIS

for Anne-Marie Moroney

When the well
of light
is bloodied,
and the way lost,
I want to be
like that ash;
at midnight
to uproot myself,
and lead my life
elsewhere.

But when words
well up in me
like tears,
I'll know
I have found
my way.

THE WOUND

I will heal this wound
by cutting deeply into it,
as if it were hardened,
neglected earth.

I will separate stones,
bits of broken glass
from dark, damp
deep earth.

When soft clay is ready
I will plant fairest flowers,
in memory
of my young self.

BOA JANUS

In Caldragh
graveyard
    you and I
    stumbled
among headstones
in August rain
    searching for
    Boa Janus.

God-heroes,
adventurers
    seeking divine
    protection—
our touch
had the power
    to open each
    other wide.

Deep in grass
and feathery fern
    we found raised
    on a plinth
identical twins
back to back,
    mouths open,
    eyes staring.

Last night
I dreamed
    you held me
    tight

and I saw Boa Janus
entire again
	the way
	we never did.

Between the heads
a socket held
	a leaf-crown-
	in-stone;
arms crossed,
long-fingered hands
	reached around
	the stone.

Either something
deep in me
	had never let
	you go—
or else time went
searching the world
	to make us
	one again.

Huge-headed,
cross-armed
	I saw
	those twins
take everything
in—
	almond-eyed,
	staring.

CONEY HALL, 1880

a true story

Emma Buchar,
new cook at Coney Hall,
warm and well fed.

Margaret Skeane,
dismissed to an outhouse,
jealous and mean.

Their master Mr. Brabazon,
friendly towards Emma,
cruel to Margaret.

She wishes she could burn
Coney Hall down
around her seducer's feet.

In cold, dark January
Emma busy cooking,
Mr. Brabazon gone out.

Margaret
creeps into the kitchen,
knocks Emma to the ground.

Cuts her head off,
drags her body
to the draw-well.

At midnight Mr. Brabazon
sees the blood smeared
from range to well.

Margaret Skeane,
sentenced to life
penal servitude.

At the Queen's Jubilee
she gets out,
lives in James Street.

I see Margaret every night
on my way home
from work.

In Coney Hall every night
Mr. Brabazon sees
a girl

cooking at the range,
and walking from the kitchen
to the well.

FEDELM'S REPLY TO MEDB

Darkness sweeps the land
when I prophesy.
Bad news for you—

relief for me.
So restless
when I cannot see.

Medb, you ask
how your royal army will fare
in Ulster.

Leaning deep into my silence
and my solitude
I reply—

my poem clear
as the mistle thrush's
song after rain.

A SHOOTING STAR

Feet wade the dark,
eyes seek light,
the sky a tree
       laden with stars.
Orion's Belt,
       the Pleiades,
like pictures
       in a gallery.

I lean right back.
       Memory sudden
as a shooting star:
       5am, how the freezing
winter nights
       woke us;
our warmth
       rocked us to sleep.

The Woody Island

That stone seat in late summer,
at the place full of rocks
high above the sea,
oh everyone knows the ruined
watch-house, it's a landmark,
but who knows the seat
at the back of the ruin,
where both of us sleep
close as possible?

Who knows the yellow hills,
hill of the sorrel,
hilltop of the furze,
the stormy hill,
hill of the fairy tree,
hill of the ridge,
the round hill of the oakwood,
hill of the two holly trees,
the cold back of a hill?

In the woods at Áine's fort
the sound of twigs snapping
wrenches us apart:
only doves nestbuilding.
The river at the rock
of the hermitage not rushing
coldly between us, we walk
beside it till a path leads us
to a bower of hazel and ash.

In the dunes at midnight,
me rooted in you like a
single stem of marram grass
swaying back and forth,
sand spreads its long
white hair
across the beach,
beacons blink out time,
time blessed for us.

House of the little church,
holm of the weir,
ford of the alders,
wood of the ancient tree,
wood of the road.
What if a wood sprang up
in every place we have slept?
We'd see this island
overflowing with trees.

Every nook and niche
we've shared
I remember vividly.
Like those dolmens scattered
all over Ireland,
those *beds of Diarmaid
and Gráinne*—
we have left our mark
everywhere.

THE STILLNESS OF TREES

Here, in this wilderness,
we learn
the stillness of trees.

From a high branch a bird
welcomes us:
'Forget the world!'

A strong, silent
presence.
It must be the trees.

I'd love to be like them,
birdsong haunting
my branches.

My spirits brighten.
Strong, silent trees
watch us leave.

And that high, hypnotic
voice calls out:
'Goodnight!'

POLL NA BPÉIST, INIS MÓR

Stare down at the pool
which fascinates you—

Poll na bPéist brings you
somewhere deep.

Let the lights in the houses
at Gort na gCapall

guide you home, scrambling
across fields of hollow stone—

the bright evening sky
shining through gaps

in the drystone walls,
like big blue stars.

for Líadan

FATHER-IN-LAW

Older-looking since you died,
fragile, you stand before me,
your shirt too big,
your chest a wound.
A small pine tree explodes into fire.
You quickly douse the flames;
then satisfied, smiling,
give me a friendly
hug, as if to say
you always liked me.
I wake up thinking about you.
Your son wears your signet ring.
Have you been watching us?
Have you seen all that's happened
since you died?

WALKING THE SEAWALL

Mirrors

1

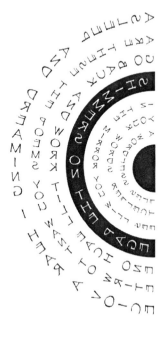

MANY SELVES

MANY THINGS A HAND CAN DO. I CAN WEAR MANY FACES. BUT IF I FIND THE RIGHT WORDS, YOU WILL SEE THE FACE I HIDE. I MET A YOUNGER SELF TODAY, HER VOICE A BIRD SKIMMING THE AIR. MY PALM OUTSTRETCHED LIKE A BEGGAR'S, IF SHE LANDS I WILL BE RICH. SHE AND I SHARE THE SAME EMPTINESS WHEN WE CANNOT FIND THE WORDS WE NEED. AND WHEN WORDS ARE GIVEN. THEN THE WORLD FALLS INTO CHAOS. BUT LIKE A SHIP WE CROSS TO A NEW SHORE, FOR A WHILE AT PEACE WITH OUR MANY SELVES.

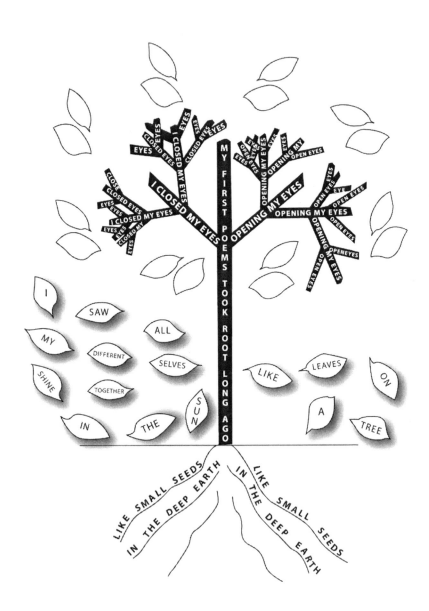

5 STEPS DOWN
A BRIGHT WELL
LIES HIDDEN
A PERFECT DEN
FOR CHILDREN

LADYWELL, SLANE

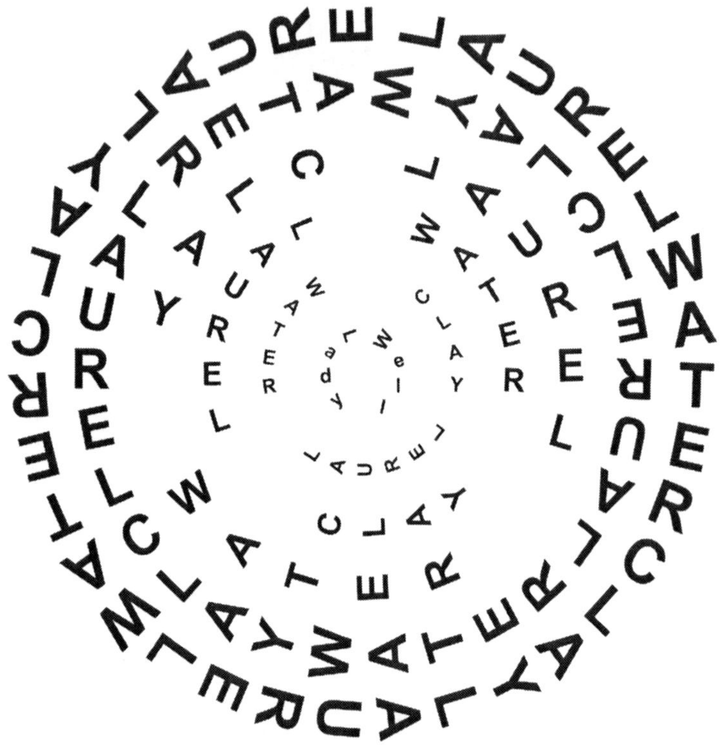

The castle gates
open,
the old path
busy all day.
People talk,
people pray.
Flower-shrine.
Amber river.
I break off
a sprig of laurel,
scoop up clay.
I dip an empty
bottle
in the well.
Bring home water
on Lady Day.

August 15th

I gcuimhne Cháitlín Bean Uí Chairbre,
Droichead Átha.

SONGS OF AMERGIN

i seek   irelan   d

i seek   irelan   d
seeki   relan   di
eekir   elan   di s
ekire   lan   di se
kirel   an   di see
irela   n   di seek
relan   di seek i
elan   di seek ir
lan   di seek ire
an   di seek irel
n   di seek irela
di seek   irelan
di seek   irelan
i seek   irelan   d
i seek   irelan
i seek   irela
i seek   irel
i seek   ire
i seek   ir
i seek   i
i seek
i see
i se
i s
i

i am ocean wave

i am	ocean	wave
mai	canoe	weave
i am	ocean	wave
aim	gone	grieve
i am	ocean	wave
aim	i can	perceive
i am	ocean	wave
mai	i shine	believe

fruitful land, fishful sea

F
FRU
FRUIT
FRUITFU
FRUIT FUL
F RUIT FU L
F R UIT F U L
F R U I T F U L
F R U I T F U L F
F R U I T F U L F I
F R U I T F U L F I S
F R U I T F U L F I S H
F R U I T F U L F I S H F
F R U I T F U L F I S H F U
F R U I T F U L F I S H F U L
FRUITFUL LAND FISHFUL SEA
FISHFUL SEA FRUITFUL LAND
F I S H F U L F R U I T F U L
F I S H F U L F R U I T F U
F I S H F U L F R U I T F
F I S H F U L F R U I T
F I S H F U L F R U I
F I S H F U L F R U
F I S H F U L F R
F I S H F U L F
F I S H F U L
F ISH F U L
FISH FU L
FISHFUL
FISHF
FIS
F

WALKING THE SEAWALL AT BALTRAY

To scramble spiderlike
  at low tide,
    over the seaweed-
slippy, barnacled
  rocks of the
    seawall,
out to the farthest
  beacon, *Aliera*,
    reminds them
they are back
  in their magic land,
    contemplating

their old world
  across the river:
    the Maiden Tower,
the mobile homes,
  the mussel
    beds,
themselves in
  another time.
    They say they'll
take a shortcut there
  some day, in a
    borrowed boat.

This other side
  is their world now,
    on their left
the beach where
  sand sinks
    knee high,
the rusty shipwreck
  glimpsed
    through a sea
of marram grass
  where they have
    lain

w r w
a i a
v v v
e e e
s r s
w r w
a i a
v v v
e e e
s r s
w r w
a i a
v v v
e e e
s r s
w r w
a i a
v v v
e e e
s r s
w r w
a i a
v v v
e e e
s r s
w r
a i a
v v v
e e e
s r s
w r w
a i a
v v v
e e e
s r s
w r w
a i a
v v v
e e e
s r s

listening to the
  swish of marram,
    its yellow tips
crackling like tiny
  swords above
    their heads.
They stand up straight
  and walk
    the seawall
as though it were
  a tightrope. Far out,
    a ship waits.

Ask them
  their favourite sight—
    they'll agree:
a ship entering
  the Boyne
    at night, led in
by the pilot boat
  at full tide,
    past cormorant-
crowned *Aliera*,
  to vanish round
    the Crook,

the wash creating
  noisy waves
    against both walls.
Then to watch
  the river
    grow still again,
a mirror for
  beacon lights
    dancing
to their own music,
  which only *they*
    can hear.

THE FIVE ROADS
AT TARA

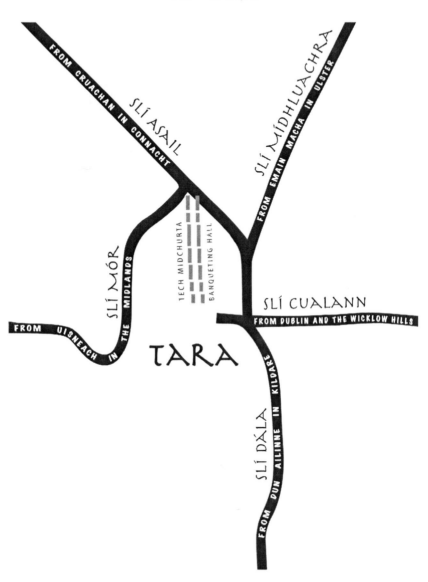

SLÍ ASAIL
FROM CRUACHAN IN CONNACHT

SLÍ MIDHLUACHRA
FROM EMAIN MACHA IN ULSTER

TECH MIDCHURTA
BANQUETING HALL

SLÍ MÓR
FROM UISNEACH IN THE MIDLANDS

SLÍ CUALANN
FROM DUBLIN AND THE WICKLOW HILLS

TARA

SLÍ DÁLA
FROM DUN AILINNE IN KILDARE

THE FIVE ROADS AT TARA

*The five great roads radiating out from Tara
reached deep into the Irish countryside.*

Slí Asail rolls down the 'chariot slope',
    past Loch Owel in Westmeath,
races towards the Shannon.
    Slí Mór strikes south to Eiscir Riada,
then heads west to Galway.

Slí Dála—the main road south,
    forges a path to Slieve Bloom.
Slí Cualann follows the Dublin road,
    spans the Liffey at the Hurdle-ford,
and on to the Hostel of Dá Derga.

My way home is by **Slí Midhluachra**,
    crossing the Boyne
at the 'Ford of Brow'.
    Slí Midhluachra plunges north,
high and deep into Ulster,

breaks free of its reins at Moyra Pass,
    gallops by Slieve Gullion
and the Dorsey: 'the gateway'—
    to Emain Macha,
and faraway Dunseverick.

CORMORANT

```
S                                       s
p d                                   s c
r r c                               s c a
e y o c                           s c a r
a   r o c                       s c a r e
d l m r o c                   s c a r e c
i i o m r o c               s c a r e c r
n k r o m r o c           s c a r e c r o
g e a r o m r o c s c a r e c r o w
    n a r o m   s c a r e c r o w
o a t n a r   s c a r e c r o w     o
u     t n   s c a r e c r o w     a f
t f i     s c a r e c r o w     i
  i s   s c a r e c r o w       s c t
h s   s c a r e c r o w   o c     o h
i h s c a r e c r o w     m r o c r e
s i c a r e c r o w     r o m r o m
  n a r e c r o w t n a r o m r o s
w g r e c r o w     t n a r o m r e
i   e c r o w       t n a r o a a
n n c r o w         t n a r n m
g e r o w           t n a t e
s t o w             t n   a
    w               t i d
t a                 s o
o                     w
```

Spreading out his wings to dry like a fishing net
a cormorant is scarecrow of the seameadow

Rose 1

```
              R
          R   O   R
      R   O   S   O   R
  R   O   S   E   S   O   R
  R   O   S   E   S   O   R
      R   O   S   O   R
          R   O   R
              R
              E  s  o  r
              S  o  r
              O  r
              R
           r  O
        r o  S
     r o s  E
              E  s  o  r
              S  o  r
              O  r
              R
           r  O
        r o  S
     r o s  E
              E  s  o  r
              S  o  r
              O  r
              R
              O
              S
              E
```

```
              R
            R O
          R O S
        R O S E

        R O S A
        R O S I E
        R O S I T A
        R O S A L I A

        R O S A L Y N
        R O S E M A R Y
        R O S A M U N D E
        M A R Y R O S E

        R O S E M A R Y
        R O S A L I A
        R O S I T A
        R O S A

          R O S E
          R O S
          R O
          R

            R O S
            S E
            E

        R O S
        S A
        A

          R O S
          I T
          A

        R O S
        A L I
        A

        R O S
        L Y
        N                         f
                                 or
        R O S E              rose-
        M A R                mary
        Y                    rosa
                             an
            R O S A          d
            M U N            m
            D E              a
                             r
        M A R Y              y
        R O S
        E                    r
                             o
            R O              s
            S E              e
```

EDEL

```
                        E

   E                                              L
                        D
            D                              E
                        E
                  E              D
                        L
                  L   edel   E
                      dele
   E      D    E   L   eled   E    D    E    L
                      lede
                  L   edel   E
                        E
                  E              D
                        D
            D                              E
                        E
   E                                              L


                        L

                        e
                        d
                        e
                        l
                        e
                        d
                        e
                        l

                        e
                        d
                        e
                        l
                        e
                        d
                        e
                        l

                        e
                        d
                        e
                        l
                        e
                        d
                        e
                        l

                        ed
                        el
```

AT A TERRY RILEY CONCERT

for Breifne

1.   2.

ALL THE THREADS
OF MY LIFE
ARE

```
              T                    W
            T  H                 W   O
          T  H  I              W   O   V
        T  H  I  S           W   O   V   E
      T  H  I  S  M        W   O   V   E   N
    T  H  I  S  M  U     W   O   V   E   N   I
  T  H  I  S  M  U  S   W  O  V  E  N  I  N
 T H I S M U S I      W O V E N I N T
T H I S M U S I C   W O V E N I N T O
S P I R A L L I N G  T H I S M U S I C
 S  P  I  R  A  L  L  I  N   T  H  I  S  M   U  S  I
  S  P  I  R  A  L  L  I     T  H  I  S  M   U  S
   S  P  I  R  A  L  L       T  H  I  S  M   U
    S  P  I  R  A  L         T  H  I  S  M
     S  P  I  R  A           T  H  I  S
      S  P  I  R             T  H  I
       S  P  I               T  H
        S  P                 T
         S
      INWARD,
   SWEEPS THROUGH
MY DREAMING SELVES
```

A WARM
WARM
WARM
ARM
RM
M

LIGHT
LIGHT
LIGHT
IGHT
GHT
HT
T

SHINES
SHINES
HINES   SHINES
INES   HINES
NES   INES
ES   NES
S   ES
        S

LIGHT
LIGHT LIGHT
IGHT GHT HT
ES

WITHIN
WITHIN ITHIN
ITHIN THIN
THIN HIN
HIN IN
IN N
N

WITHIN
THIN
HIN
IN
N

A WARM
WARM
WARM
ARM
RM
M

WITHIN S ES NES
HINES
INES
SHINES

ST. STEPHEN'S NIGHT

late St. Stephen's night
naked near the fire
can you feel my heat
and my sorrow?
I remember
lying down
with you
on the
floor
of this
sleeping
world and
when we came
I felt your heat
and your sorrow
naked near the fire
late St. Stephen's night

Sandwaves

```
        s                           w
       s a                         w a
      s a s a                     w a w a
     s a n s a n                 w a v w a v
    s a n d s a n d             w a v e w a v e
   s a n d w s a n d           w a v e s w a v e
  s a n d w a s a n d         w a v e s a w a v e
 s a n d w a v s a n d       w a v e s a n w a v e
s a n d w a v e s a n d w a v e s a n d w a v e
s a n d w a v e s a n d w a v e s a n d w a v e
 s a n d w a v s a n d       w a v e s a n w a v e
  s a n d w a s a n d         w a v e s a w a v e
   s a n d w s a n d           w a v e s w a v e
    s a n d s a n d             w a v e w a v e
     s a n s a n                 w a v w a v
      s a s a                     w a w a
       s a                         w a
        s                           w
        s                           w
       s a                         w a
      s a s a                     w a w a
     s a n s a n                 w a v w a v
    s a n d s a n d             w a v e w a v e
   s a n d w s a n d           w a v e s w a v e
  s a n d w a s a n d         w a v e s a w a v e
 s a n d w a v s a n d       w a v e s a n w a v e
s a n d w a v e s a n d w a v e s a n d w a v e
s a n d w a v e s a w a n d v e s a n d w a v e
 s a n d w a v w a v e       s a n d s a n w a v e
  s a n d w a v e w a         n d s a n d w a v e
   s w a v e w a v e           s a n d s a n d e
    w a v e w a v e             s a n d s a n d
     w a v w a v                 s a n s a n
      w a w a                     s a s a
       w a                         s a
        w                           s
```

94

```
        s                  w
        s a                w a
        s a s a            w a w a
        s a n s a n        w a v w a v
      s a n d s a n d  w a v e w a v e
      s a n d w s a n wd a v e s w a v e
      s a n d w a s a wn ad v e s a w a v e
    s a n d w a v s wa an vd e s a n w a v e
  s a n d w a v e ws aa vn ed s a n d w a v e
  w a v e s a n d sw aa nv de w a v e s a n d
    w a v e s a n w sa av ne d w a v s a n d
    w a v e s a w a sv ae n d w a s a n d
      w a v e s w a v se a n d w s a n d
      w a v e w a v e s a n d s a n d
        w a v w a v        s a n s a n
        w a w a            s a s a
        w a                s a
        w                  s
```

sandwaves racing past us
down the windswept beach
gather round the marker
as far as we will go

HAIKU

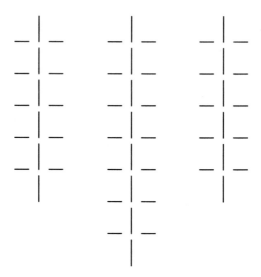

MONASTERBOICE

Monasterboice lies close to the M1 motorway, five miles north of Drogheda, Co. Louth. Once a mediaeval monastery, its round tower catches the eye of the passer-by and marks the place of two elaborately carved High Crosses from the 9th century. These are known as the Cross of Muiredach and the West or Tall Cross and stand 5.5 metres and 7 metres high respectively. The former monastery is today a well-cared-for cemetery.

The east and west face of each cross is divided into panels in which various episodes from the bible are carved. The centre of the west face bears the Crucifixion. Their sides are covered with panels of interlace, possibly painted long ago, and reminiscent of the Book of Kells. The panel of the Dextera Dei or Hand of God carved under the northern arm of the Cross of Muiredach stretches out in blessing and protection over the person standing below.

In their time these scripture crosses were places where people gathered to learn about the gospel scenes from the life of Christ. Because of their age and a millennium's exposure to the elements, some of the panels are now difficult to decipher. However, walking around the Cross of Muiredach on a winter's afternoon when the sun is low and shadows deep, one can clearly see the expression on Christ's face: sad, serious, serene.

THE CROSS OF MUIREDACH

Tall
cross
crowned
with a miniature
prayer-house.

Christ
faces west.
His feet are bound.
Two angels support his head,
sun and moon
eclipsed.

Worn expressions
come to life
at sunset—
sad, serious,
serene.

Two
sandstone
cats
sunbathe
below
chiselled words:
or do Muiredach —
'a prayer for Muiredach
who had this cross made.'

THE WEST CROSS

1.

weather
worn
all over
like a
s
  i
   l
    v
     e
      r
viking
coin —
the west cross
i s
a
p
i
 c
  t
   u
    r
     e-
book
in stone
where I find
C
 h
  r
   i
    s
     t
walking
the
 s
  e
   a

2.

in
this
quiet
shady
graveyard
n
a
 m
  e
   s
d
a
t
e
 s
tell
their story —
still
r
a
d
 i
  a
   t
    e
and
r
e
 c
  e
   i
    v
     e
love

Dextera Dei

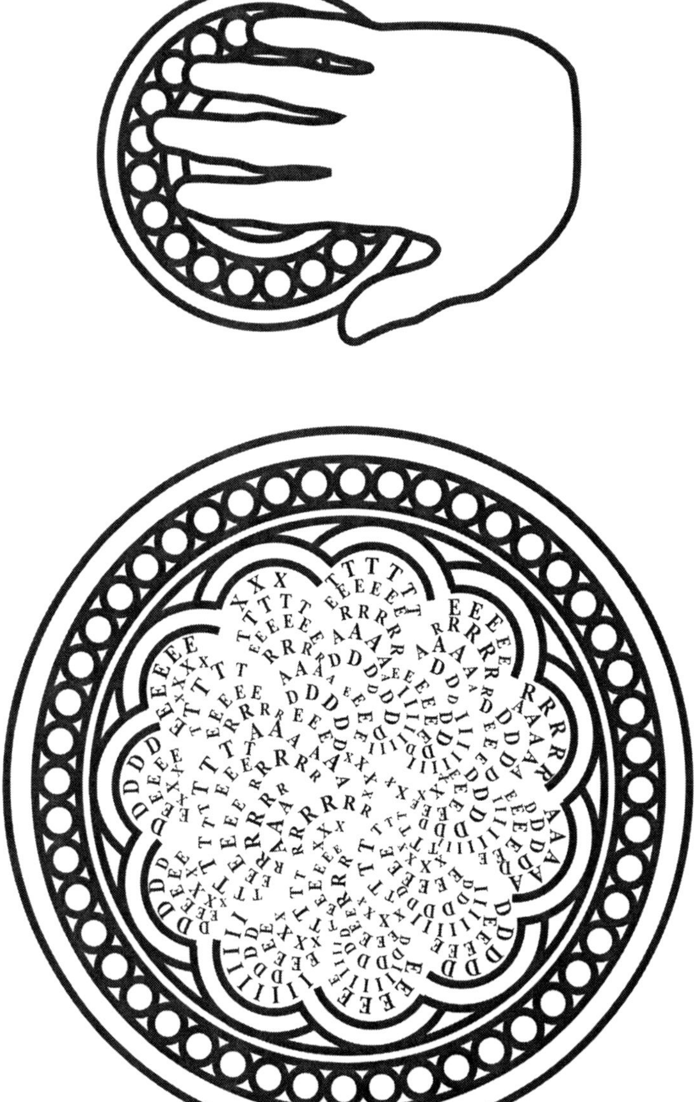

Names for a High Cross

```
                t
              t   a
            t   a   l
          t   a   l   l
        t   a   l   l   t
      t   a   l   l   t   a
    t   a   l   l   t   a   l
  t   a   l   l   t   a   l   l
t   a   l   l   t   a   l   l   t
  t   a   l   l   t   a   l   l   t   a
    t   a   l   l   t   a   l   l   t   a   l
  w       t   a   l   l   t   a   l   l   t   a   l   l              w
we        t   a   l   l   t   a   l   l   t   a          wo
wes       t   a   l   l   t   a   l   l   t           wor
west      t   a   l   l   t   a   l   l         worn
westw     t   a   l   l   t   a   l        worn w
westwe    t   a   l   l   t   a         worn wo
westwes   t   a   l   l   t        worn wor
westwest  t   a   l   l         worn worn
westwestw t   a   l        worn worn w
westwestwe t   a        worn worn wo
westwestwes t        worn worn wor
westwestwest         worn worn worn
westwestwes    h     worn worn wor
westwestwe    h  i   worn worn wo
westwestw     h  i  g   worn worn w
westwest      h  i  g  h   worn worn
westwes      h  i  g  h  h   worn wor
westwe      h  i  g  h  h  i   worn wo
westw       h  i  g  h  h  i  g   worn w
west       h  i  g  h  h  i  g  h   worn
wes       h  i  g  h  h  i  g  h  h   wor
we       h  i  g  h  h  i  g  h  h  i   wo
w       h  i  g  h  h  i  g  h  h  i  g              w
       h  i  g  h  h  i  g  h  h  i  g  h
        h  i  g  h  h  i  g  h  h  i  g
         h  i  g  h  h  i  g  h  h  i
          h  i  g  h  h  i  g  h  h
           h  i  g  h  h  i  g  h
            h  i  g  h  h  i  g
             h  i  g  h  h  i
              h  i  g  h  h
               h  i  g  h
                h  i  g
                 h  i
                  h
```

high	tall	worn	west
tall	worn	west	high
worn	west	high	tall
west	high	tall	worn

CHRIST IN THE ARMS OF THIS CROSS

```
                        C
                    C       H
                C       H       R
            C       H       R       I
        C       H       R       I       S
    C       H       R       I       S       T
    i       H       R       I       S       T       a
  in the        R       I       S       T       arms o
 in the in the        I       S       T       arms of arm
in the in the in the        S       T       arms of arms of ar
in the in the in the in the        T       arms of arms of arms of
in the in the in the in the in the        arms of arms of arms of arm
in the in the in the in the        C       arms of arms of arms of
in the in the in the        C       R       arms of arms of ar
   this this this        C       R       O       arms of arm
    this thi        C       R       O       S       arms o
        t       C       R       O       S       S       a

            C       R       O       S       S
                R       O       S       S
                    O       S       S
                    S       S
                        S
```

Around the Cross

Printed in the United Kingdom
by Lightning Source UK Ltd.
136063UK00001B/64-75/P